Introduction

The goldfish, known scientifically as *Carassius auratus*, is probably the most popular cold water aquarium fish in the world. This is really not surprising as it was the FIRST fish to be domesticated. Its history goes back to about the 11th Century when it was selectively bred by the Chinese—initially as a food source, but later for its beauty. When it was noticed that an orange form of the local version of the otherwise rather drab looking species that is related to or identical with *Carassius carassius* (the Crucian carp) began to appear in captive stock, this aroused much interest. The Chinese were astute enough to realize that this new color form could be retained by careful breeding.

It became fashionable for wealthy people to keep a goldfish in ponds and later in all manner

◆ Common goldfish are raised by the billions on a worldwide basis. Many are sold as *feeder goldfish* which means they are fed to larger aquarium fishes. The scientific name is *Carassius auratus*.

◆The Crucian carp, *Carassius carassius*, is the wild ancestor of domesticated goldfish.

▲ An old Japanese lithograph showing a mother nursing her son in the presence of a goldfish. Goldfish and carp were used as examples of endurance and dedication...and they still are to this day!

▲ A nursing mother tending her child in the presence of both goldfish and canaries. Perhaps the child is a girl and she wants the child to be a singer?

of vessels. With the passage of time the orange form was improved to become red, while an albino form appeared as well. Soon there were multicolored varieties and it was found that specimens with unusual fins were beginning to appear. The hobby of fishkeeping for esthetic reasons only had begun.

The Chinese developed a number of varieties of goldfish and many were exported. By AD 1500 the goldfish had arrived in Japan, where it was to be subject to the special breeding skills of this nation during the next few centuries. Unlike the Chinese, whose tastes border the grotesque in terms of fish body development, the

From the goldfish, *Carassius auratus*, the Japanese developed the Pearl Scale goldfish and as well as many ➤ other varieties.

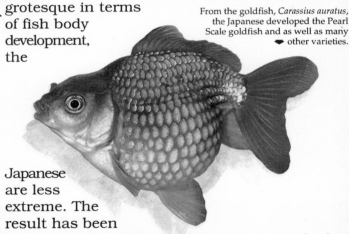

Japanese are less extreme. The result has been a number of very beautiful varieties. By the late 17th Century the goldfish was exported to Europe where it attracted tremendous interest wherever it was seen. During the 19th century the goldfish arrived in both the U.S.A. and in Australia. In the U.S.A. further varieties were developed so that today the aquarist may choose from over 100 types. However, for the average person thinking of keeping these fish the choice will be from one of only a few varieties. Many of the others are either rarely, if ever, seen outside of the Orient, or are rather delicate and not recommended to any but the most experienced of keepers.

The goldfish has proved a popular fish for a number of reasons. Preeminent in these is the fact that it is very durable. It has survived more by its own ability to live under adverse conditions than for any skills displayed by its owners to provide adequate accommodation over the centuries. In spite of its inborn

toughness the sad fact is that millions of these little fish die each year because they are not given the needed care that any fish must have. The goldfish is a ready breeder and this too has

An early aquarium (in the background) with a hand operated water spray. From an ancient Japanese lithograph.

Women discussing the powers of goldfish and koi...and the effect they have on their boys. From an ancient Japanese lithograph.

A Japanese mother telling her son to imitate the qualities of a goldfish (carp). These fish are famous in the Orient for their endurance, persistence and ability to survive under difficult conditions.

helped it maintain its popularity. It has been bred in such numbers that its cost has always been low when compared to other aquarium fish.

Unlike tropical fish, which need careful attention to matters such as water temperature and filtration, the goldfish is much more able to withstand a range of conditions. However, this does not mean this is desirable: by supplying ideal living conditions it will be found that the goldfish will live a longer and happier life. Its colors will also show themselves to far better effect than they will under poor conditions. In this book you will be given advice on all matters related to sound aquatic husbandry. This will enable you to obtain far greater enjoyment from

◀ This woodcut from 1864 shows the Japanese goldfish vendor. Superimposed are two modern Japanese goldfish showing the egg-shaped body as the Calico shown above possesses.

➨ A later Japanese development was the Fringetail with the split tail fin. The name *fringetail* was later changed to Veiltail.

🖝 Europeans had their silly customs like *touching a chimneysweep for good luck*; the Japanese and Chinese are very superstitious about goldfish and carp. Thus a goldfish vendor brought good luck. Keeping and eating carp or goldfish is also considered lucky, especially for young boys entering school or studying for an important examination.

☚ The Chinese breeds of goldfish deal mainly with absurd body forms like this Water Bubble Eye. The bubbles on the eyes of this fish are filled with lymph and become so heavy that the fish can hardly raise itself from the bottom of the aquarium. They could not survive in an outside pool.

these delightful fish. With due care to their accommodation you will begin to see why the goldfish has maintained its position as the world's most popular pet cold water fish and why it is gaining more and more specialist devotees.

☚ Going *modern*, this Japanese housewife has a ceramic goldfish bowl the inside surface of which is painted with illustrations of fancy goldfish. These bowls are still being manufactured and are available at stores featuring ornamental Oriental pottery.

◀ Japanese school girls collecting goldfish which escaped from a goldfish farm when flooding washed out the banks of the breeding ponds.

☚ An 18th Century woodcut from Japan depicting a special *medicine man* who uses a mask to frighten evil spirits while he uses goldfish to bring luck and good health.

1. The Aquatic Environment

Top, facing page: A more expensive goldfish pool can be dug into the ground and, using forms, made of cement. The walls of the pond should protrude 24 inches out of the ground to insure that no one falls in.

In order to fully appreciate how best to provide your goldfish with a really satisfactory home it is useful to consider the natural environment in which fish live. If this can be duplicated, and the potential dangers removed, it would seem reasonable to assume this will make for a good home.

The goldfish is a freshwater species, as compared with those that live in saltwater—the marine fish. The two types are very different in the way their metabolisms work. Goldfish live in slow moving waters where they feed at the middle to bottom levels of rivers and ponds. This is evident by the position of the mouth. It is called terminal but slightly inferior, meaning it is at the front end of the head but just slightly below the mid line.

Fish breathe by extracting oxygen from the water via their gills, so the oxygen content of water is important to fish. This is not always

◗ A simple goldfish pond can be dug in your backyard. Plastic liners or sunken baby pool waders are good enough PROVIDING the water they contain does NOT freeze solid during the winter. Be sure to put a fence around it so people or animals don't fall in at night.

appreciated by those new to fishkeeping. The oxygen is gotten from the atmosphere and dissolves in the water at its surface. The upper levels of the water are thus those richest in oxygen. The lower levels of any body of water gain their oxygen by slow diffusion of the gas, or by the water being agitated such that the lower levels are brought to the surface. This happens when rivers pass over waterfalls, or form eddies when they pass over rocks. Fast rivers will tend to contain more oxygen than slow rivers.

Debris, as well as the fecal matter and urine of fish, is kept to a low level in rivers both by the natural bacteria that live on debris, and by the fact that the river is always on the move toward the sea. Inland lakes are fed by mountain streams while rivers (surface or underground) take the lake water on to the open oceans. Natural waters that support life are thus always moving. As they do so they pass over rocks and soils, dissolving these. The minerals in the rocks are thus an important component of fresh water, but again are kept in balance by the ever moving water so they never build up to dangerous proportions.

Likewise, the population of fish in any body of water is always such that it stays in ratio with the amount of oxygen present and the amount of food available. If the population increases too much then the number that die from disease or lack of food increases. Water commences its cycle by falling as rain onto mountains. This is very pure at first but as it travels ever downwards and onwards it dissolves whatever it passes over and accumulates whatever debris is placed into it. Rain replenishes that lost from

☛ An elaborate fountain system can be installed in your goldfish pond...limited only by your imagination and pocketbook.

☛ A natural goldfish pond can be dug and lined with clay or plastic and then planted with lovely water and bog plants to become a natural body of water with beautiful consequences.

surface evaporation, but how pure the rain is obviously depends on the state of cleanliness of the air it falls through. The temperature of the water varies according to its depth. The water near the surface is more prone to fluctuation than that at the lower depths, which remains remarkably constant providing there is sufficient depth. When the river surface freezes that below does not, so the fish will seek the deeper levels during the winter months. There they will stay almost motionless in a state

of semi-hibernation. In this way they use little energy and so do not need to feed until the springtime when the warmer weather arrives. Goldfish do, however, eat under most cold water conditions. If you consider all the important aspects of a natural body of water you will appreciate that an aquarium is actually a far from ideal place for your fish to live in. This being so, you must try to overcome the negatives such that you compensate for their shortcomings. The main aspects that must be compensated for are:

▲ This is the wonderful RT30 (RiverTank System, 30 gallons) which combines a goldfish tank, a reptile area and plants. The fish can move from side to side via pools at different levels which are connected by rapids and waterfalls. The plants grow hydroponically from a hidden gravel pocket in the rear of the goldfish tank. This also acts as a biological filter device.

1. Water in a container will not be moving so must be made to do so—or it must be replaced on a reasonably regular basis.

2. Impurities in the water must be removed so that what remains is at an acceptable level.

3. The temperature must be controlled so that it remains within acceptable limits.

4. The population in the aquarium must be controlled such that it has sufficient oxygen.

If these four major aspects are managed correctly then the result will be an environment in which the fish will be seen at their best. They will be living under nearly ideal conditions. By the use of aeration and filtration technology in a basic form, coupled with aquascaping (the addition of rocks, plants and other decorative features), you can create a natural environment that is in many ways superior to that in which the fish would ordinarily live.

Choosing an Aquarium

In choosing a container in which to house your goldfish you will no doubt be bounded by at least some constraints. These will include the cost, the number of fish you may wish to own, the space available, and any decoration you might like to feature within the container. A visit to one or more pet or aquatic stores will show you just what a vast range of aquariums you can pick from—so how do you decide which will be the best for a given sum of money? The first advice is that you should always select the largest aquarium you can afford. Do not be swayed by fancy shapes, they will cost more money and are less satisfactory in most instances.The classic rectangular shape still remains the best option. On no account should you consider purchasing the old fashioned goldfish globe which is totally unsuitable to house any fish. From what was discussed in the

This goldfish tank won first prize at a local aquarium show. The beautiful Lionhead goldfish have lovely caps on their heads and they are, of course, without dorsal fins. The Japanese ceramic ornaments and large plastic plants don't leave a lot of free swimming room for the Lionhead goldfish.

last chapter it will be appreciated that the total water surface area is very important. It is here that oxygen dissolves. The number of fish that can be kept will be controlled by the oxygen content – which is why the old narrow-necked

Plastic aquariums are a necessity as isolation tanks for new arrivals or as a maternity ward. ▶

Complete plastic aquariums, with fitted hoods, are available. This one is a *Hagen Living World TropiQuarium.*

Hagen makes a wide range of aquarium products including a complete aquarium starter kit which contains almost everything you need to get started. Just add water, plants, fishes and a proper stand or table. ▶

Tanks should be longer than they are tall to ensure a proper exchange of oxygen and carbon dioxide at the water's surface. ▶

If you already have a tank, your dealer can offer a Hagen starter kit which has most of the necessities. These kits are usually cheaper than buying the items separately.

bowls are poor containers because they allow little oxygen to be dissolved unless they are half empty. The rectangular shape not only provides a good surface to volume area, but also provides good viewing. It does not distort the look of the fish as does a circular shape, and it allows you to decorate the aquarium more attractively. Finally, it is better suited to accommodating air, filter and lighting equipment, which can be discreetly hidden behind plants and rocks.

➤ Discuss with a knowledgeable dealer the costs of the largest tank possible. Remember your tank needs a cover (hood), heater, filter, plants and fishes, as well as a stand upon which to place it.

This goldfish bowl is NOT satisfactory for more than one small goldfish or a large male Siamese Fighting Fish. ▶

A small flat goldfish bowl is preferred to a long, tall one because it gets more oxygen.

Your selection of an aquarium stand depends upon the furniture in your home and the cost. The ideal is a closed cabinet in which paraphernalia can be stored out of sight. ➤

Make sure that the aquarium fits perfectly on the aquarium stand. This should be done BEFORE you buy the tank and stand.

One manufacturer makes a plexiglas tank with a fitted canopy and stand which is beautiful but very expensive. ▶

The Number of Fish

The number of fish you can keep in your aquarium is dependent on their size and the surface area of the water. The calculations are based on your being able to accommodate 2.5 cm (1 in) of fish body (excluding the tail) for every 150 cm^2 (24 in^2) of water surface. The depth of water is important only insofar as it gives the fish more room in which to swim around—and the more they have, the better they will be. When calculating how many fish a given tank will hold remember that you will probably purchase young fish and these will grow to twice or more times their initial size.

If the aquarium is 46 x 31cm (18 x 12 in) in length and width then its surface area is 46 x 31 = 1426 cm^2. If this is divided by 150 and the result multiplied by 2.5 this will give the total body length of fish it can accommodate.

1426 divided by 150 = 9.51 x 2.5 = 24 cm of fish.

This would allow you to keep three goldfish each of 7.5 cm (3 in) or two at this length plus two of 4.5 cm (1.75 in) approximately. This assumes the aquarium receives no additional oxygen supplied by mechanical means (air pump) or by a filtration system. It should be mentioned that the amount of oxygen in the water is affected by the temperature—the warmer the water the less oxygen it can hold. Assuming your fish are to be kept in a room that is normally heated to about 65°F (18°C), you are advised to stay safely within the theoretical total size limit.

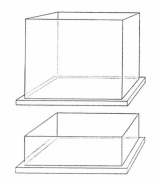

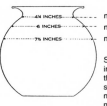

4¼ INCHES — makes 14 square inches of surface
6 INCHES — makes 28 square inches of surface
7¾ INCHES — makes 44 square inches of surface

Surprising how rapidly the surface increases as the water lowers from the top of a globe. The bottom level shown will support three times as many fishes as the top, and the middle one twice as many. The matter of how far a globe is filled may make the difference between failure and success.

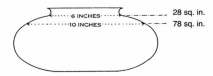

6 INCHES — 28 sq. in.
10 INCHES — 78 sq. in.

The modern flattened globe has a lot more style and very much more air-contact surface, especially when carried a little below the top level.

12 INCHES — 113 sq. in.

The main intent of these diagrams is to show the practical application of the all important air-surface principle.

These three containers are reduced in the same proportion and each has approximately the same water capacity. As an aquarium the lower design is much the best. Theoretically, when filled, it could support eight times as many fishes as the top globe filled. In practice the old style globes are almost always overcrowded, and the thing to do is to take goldfish from these and place them in better-formed aquaria. However, owners of flat-shaped aquaria are not to be encouraged in the possible idea that they would be justified in increasing their aquarium population just because the old-style globe is less efficient.

This is an RT10 (River Tank System, 10 gallons capacity and ideal for a few small goldfish). It is an exciting innovation in goldfish aquariums. It simulates the action of an actual slow moving river by creating a living ecosystem. The goldfish move from pool to pool and the water trickles through a hidden gravel pocket in the rear which becomes a biological filter that provides nutrients for the plants.

Water Volume & Weight

You will need to know the volume of water your tank holds because this will be of some importance should you add medicines. It will be needed to determine the size of pump you use, if you plan to include one, and in order to calculate the weight of the unit once it is filled up (and maybe placed onto a shelf). The volume is obtained by multiplying the length by the width by the depth. Most aquariums these days state their volume on the packaging. Let us assume the aquarium is 45 x 30 x 30 cm (18 x 12 x 12 in) then its volume will be: 45 x 30 x 30 = 40,500 cm³. There are 3,785 cm³ in a US gallon, so if this is divided into the volume you will have the number of gallons—in this case there being 10.7. The British gallon is equal to 1.2 US gallons so if the US figure is divided by 1.2 this will give a British volume of 8.9 gallons. The US gallon is equal to 3.8 liters so the tank will hold 41 liters (approximately). No tank is ever filled to the brim, and furnishings will displace water, so the practical capacity will be somewhat less than its actual capacity.

A US gallon of water weighs 8.35 lb (3.8 kg)

while that of the UK weighs 10 lb (4.55 kg), so it is easy to multiply by the volume to obtain the weight of the water. You must then allow for the weight of the aquarium and its furnishings. Gravel used as a substrate will weigh approximately 1 lb per 283 cm^3.

Aquarium Material

The best material for an aquarium is glass but this will be more expensive than those made from molded plexiglas. However, the latter have improved dramatically over recent years and do not scratch as badly, nor turn as yellow as their counterparts of yesteryear. For the average pet goldfish owner the molded tanks are excellent as first time aquariums. Many come complete with a canopy (hood) which is to be recommended on any aquarium regardless of whether or not lights are to be fitted under it. You should also obtain an aquarium cover glass, which is fitted in order to reduce evaporation, prevent fish from jumping out (which the canopy will also do) and to reduce the amount of debris that can fall onto the water surface.

It is not at all essential that an initial aquarium set up be expensive, for the great advantage of goldfish is that they can be accommodated in basic aquariums, provided you do not attempt to keep too many—when problems are more likely to ensue if no adequate filtration system is installed.

AAM ©

▲ The top-of-the-line in aquariums is this acrylic tank manufactured by the American Acrylic Manufacturing Co. These tanks are made with bubble-eye windows and come complete with filters, pumps and all the extras that any goldfish hobbyist would want.

Aeration & Filtration

Although you do not need to either aerate or filter your aquarium, the advantages of so doing are numerous. Not to do so means you will create more work for yourself and will not see the aquarium, thus the fish, at its best. The principle advantage of these two processes is that they maintain the water to a high standard of quality. This is beneficial to the fish. The secondary advantages are that the water will stay much clearer than would otherwise be the case, the temperature remains more constant at all depths, and you can increase the stocking level of the aquarium.

The last aspect should be practiced with due caution. If the equipment breaks down, or if there is a power failure, the increased number of fish may struggle to breath. Only use aeration and filtration to increase stock levels when you have some experience in fishkeeping and have spare back-up aquariums to cope with the potential problem of equipment failure.

▶ This acrylic aquarium, on a steel stand, is made by American Acrylic. It has a 1000 gallon capacity with a double bull nose and complete cabinetry. Using acrylics, your choice of goldfish tanks is almost unlimited. These tanks can be ordered through your local pet shop.

Aeration

Additional air, thus oxygen, can be supplied to your aquarium via a small electric air pump purchased from your pet store. You can obtain piston pumps, but most hobbyists these days use one of the excellent diaphragm types, of which there are many models from inexpensive to the deluxe types. They work in the following manner. Air is sent through a pipe, the end of which is fitted into an air stone. This is made of a porous material so it releases the air as a series of tiny bubbles. As the bubbles rise and reach the surface they burst. In so doing they create tiny waves and these effectively increase the water surface to air interface—thus allowing more oxygen to be dissolved. At the same time, the rising bubbles create a partial vacuum behind them, thus a current, and so draw water upwards. The airstone is placed on the substrata, so the current takes poorly oxygenated water to the surface, while the oxygen rich surface water is taken down to the lower levels. The rate of air (thus number of bubbles) can be controlled by valves or clamps in the piping, or by a knob on the more sophisticated pumps. Note that it is the water surface agitation created that increases the oxygen content and not the bubbles, few of which will actually burst as they rise. The upward current also takes unwanted carbon dioxide (the result of fish and plant respiration) and free ammonia to the surface

There are wonderful varieties of vibrator pumps at your local pet shop. This Hagen line is internationally available. Vibrator pumps are so called because they operate on a vibrating membrane principle.

Small vibrator pumps can only operate a single bottom filter.

Hagen has a series of more powerful vibrators with outside adjustments,too.

An efficient type of filtration is WET-DRY FILTRATION based upon bacterial activity plus mechanical filtration. It works wonderfully well without making changes of filter medium.

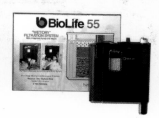

Your pet shop has an air pump that works on batteries.

The most powerful filters are called *CANISTER FILTERS*. Ask your pet shop to show you a Fluval.

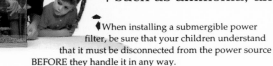

When installing a submergible power filter, be sure that your children understand that it must be disconnected from the power source BEFORE they handle it in any way.

where it dissipates into the atmosphere. There are many airstones to choose from, including those that send up a small 'curtain' of bubbles. Do not create excessive oxygen in your aquarium as goldfish will not like this. If you see bubbles forming on the leaves of plants or on rocks then you have saturated the water and this is dangerous to your fish. Reduce the air supply and the fish will get over the problem (akin to bends in divers) within a day or two. The pump should be located about a foot above the water level to overcome the problem of back siphoning should the pump fail. Alternatively, you could fit it with a one way valve or an anti-siphon tube—either of which your pet or aquatic store will have in stock.

Filtration

Although an aerator is beneficial it will do little to improve or maintain the quality of the water. For this you will need a filter system which will also do the job of aeration to a greater or lesser degree depending on the system used. There are three types of filter media.

1. MECHANICAL. This will remove solid debris from the water. Special nylon floss, or charcoal or foam, from your pet dealer is recommended. In each instance the filter prevents the debris from passing through it, so it collects on the medium which is periodically removed and cleaned.

2. CHEMICAL. Examples are activated charcoal and zeolite. They will adsorb gases, such as ammonia, and some chemicals that would pass through the average mechanical filter. These they will neutralize. Once

▶ Every aquarium must have a hood or canopy on top. This keeps the tank clean, houses the light, prevents evaporation and prevents the fish from jumping out. Photo courtesy of Hagen.

◀ The hood or canopy should fit the tank perfectly and should be purchased at the same time you buy your tank.

◀ If you cannot affort a hood, get a hinged glass top upon which you can add a light.

saturated they must be replaced or cleaned (zeolite) otherwise they will cease working as filters. They will also neutralize many medicines so must be removed when an aquarium is treated.

3. BIOLOGICAL. Certain bacteria are beneficial to aquariums because they break down waste products (uneaten food, feces,dead plants and microorganisms) into simple compounds that are used by plants as food, or which can be removed by chemical filtration. These bacteria colonize rocks, plants, the gravel and even mechanical filters. They need a good oxygen supply in order to survive.

Filter media are placed into boxes or canisters and a pump draws water from the aquarium and passes it through a filter chamber. The filtered water is then returned to the aquarium via a pipe or by a spray bar—so that it agitates the water and thus aerates it. There are many filter systems to choose from. Some are internal to the aquarium but most are external so that cleaning is made easier. You can purchase simple air-lift filters

◀ Undergravel filters must fit the exact size of the aquarium bottom. Measure it before you buy it. There are many different styles and sizes; follow the suggestions of your aquatic dealer.

To solve the problem of variable sized aquarium bottoms, Hagen developed a wonderful system of small grids which interlock and can be composed to fit any size aquarium. ◀

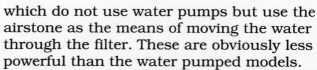

which do not use water pumps but use the airstone as the means of moving the water through the filter. These are obviously less powerful than the water pumped models.

➥ There are round undergravel filters that are made to fit goldfish globes. If you insist on a goldfish bowl, at least use an undergravel filter with it.

Goldfish are notorious for devouring plants in small aquariums but you can still have the benefit of plant biological action by pumping the water through a tank containing plants and then returning it via spray bars. You can also fit an undergravel filter to your aquarium. This works on the principle that water is drawn down through the gravel, through a filter plate and thence is returned to the surface. It supplies bacteria living on the gravel with a good oxygen supply. The water is circulated through the gravel by placing an air supply under the filter tube or by using a power head to draw the water from under the filter, then spraying it back over the surface.

➥ Clear-Flow undergravel filters come in many sizes. Their filtering power can be greatly enhanced with a powerhead.

◀ Powerheads attached to the aerating column can increase the movement through the filter by 10 times or more.

Setting Up the Aquarium

In an ideal situation you will not set up your aquarium and stock it at one and the same time. It is better that you mature the tank water and plants before fish are introduced. However, with the smaller aquarium it is probable that you wish to have a complete set up straight away, in which case the procedure is as follows.

Location

Select a site that is light yet not exposed to direct sunlight. This would result in the rapid build-up of unsightly colonies of green algae. It would also result in dramatic fluctuations in the water temperature, the moreso in a small aquarium. Do not locate near heaters as this will also bring about the same temperature rise. Keep the aquarium out of drafts, such as opposite doors. If the aquarium is to be placed on a shelf, bear in mind the total weight involved, and be sure it can withstand it.

Preparation of the Aquarium

Place a layer of polyurethane sponge sheeting under the aquarium in order to iron out any unevenness of the surface, which would otherwise place a strain on one area of the aquarium base. Give the tank a good wash down to remove any collected dust in it; do likewise with any other materials that are to be placed into the aquarium. Gravel should be well washed; leaving it overnight to soak before being rinsed would be a good idea. Prepare some conditioned tap water the day before by filling one or two buckets, agitating it and leaving it overnight in a darkened place. This will allow any chlorine

➤ You should always buy the largest size aquarium you can afford. Goldfish, under proper care and feeding, just keep on growing. It would be terrible if the goldfish outgrew the tank.

➤ Tetra Min® food for all tropical fish is great for goldfish too. Tetra makes a goldfish food as well, but I alternate the two foods and have had wonderful results.

← The clarity and purity of the water in your goldfish aquarium can be maintained with the regular use of filter box carbon. It even removes water stains.

▶ Blue Ribbon *Exotic Ornaments* include these life-like castles which enhance the decorative value of a goldfish aquarium.

to dissipate into the air. Use hot water.

If the aquarium is of reasonable size it is wise to plan the layout of the furnishings (rocks, driftwood, gravel, filter and plants), before actually setting up the unit. This can be done by drawings or by placing the furnishings (not the gravel) into the empty aquarium. If a canopy with a light in it is to be featured check that it is working and located near a power socket—which will also be needed for the filter system or aerator. Be sure wiring is not excessively long— keep it neat as this is the safest way.

Decoration (Aquascaping)

Today, you have a great choice when it comes to aquarium furnishings. You can aquascape your aquarium to hundreds of themes. You may purchase Chinese type ornaments, such as Pagodas or Lions, or you could plan a sunken city theme based on Aztec-like ornaments, or you may wish to plan a castle theme. If novelty themes do not appeal to you, then you could plan a natural type scene using rocks, driftwood, terraces and plants. These look really great and will show off your fish to best effect. As goldfish

are rather destructive to plants you can purchase imitation ones and some of these are of a very high quality, all but indistinguishable from the real thing. Bark, logs, and rocks can all be man made items that are inert yet very effective. Although colored gravels are available it is always best to use natural colors as these will not compete with your fish and will blend in much better in the aquascene you create. To be sure gravel and other materials are safe, buy them from your pet or aquatic dealer rather than taking them from ponds—which may carry many bacteria or the eggs of dangerous parasites. You can purchase murals, which are placed on the back panel of the tank, and these can look very effective.

☛ Obviously this is a posed photo. But keep in mind that goldfish are trapped in an aquarium. They are easy prey for cats or any other predator that can have access to them.

This is a Fantail goldfish. As these fish get older, their fins get longer. They have a double tail and are variously marked. These are hardy, inexpensive goldfish.

Goldfish Varieties

Although there are well over 100 goldfish varieties, this text is restricted to those that you are likely to see in the average pet or aquatic shop. These are the most beautiful forms, so you are not missing out on the more exotic types, which are more grotesque (depending on your views) and also more demanding in their requirements.

Goldfish can be seen in three scale types. Actually, all scales are the same, it being a case that the reflective layer of tissue below the scales gives the scales the appearance of being different.

Metallic scales exhibit full reflection of the colors in the upper layers of the skin. They are thus very polished or glittery in appearance. Typical colors are orange, red, yellow, white, blue, brown, and black, alone or in combination. Nacreous (Calico) scales have part of the reflective layer missing so that they have a mother-of-pearl appearance. They may also have some metallic scales present. The colors seen in these fish are the same as those in metallics. The matt scales have no reflective tissue so the fish appear not to have scales and are sometimes called leather

Telescope eyed goldfish are now fairly common. They come with and without dorsal fins and in various colors including solid black.

A 200 year old Japanese antique pin from gold and silver, featuring colored stones, depicts a telescope-eyed goldfish.

A young Lionhead with its hood just developing features a double tail and no dorsal fin.

scales. All colors mentioned are possible in this type.

When selecting your goldfish pick one of the hardy varieties that have no undue exaggeration of their fins. The common goldfish, the shubunkins, the comet, or the fantails are good ones to start with. If you start with the more fancy types and mix these with hardy varieties the latter may nip their fins, especially in small aquariums. Long finned fish are always more prone to fin problems so it is wise to gain experience with those suggested, and then try the others once you know how anxious you are to add more goldfish—and maybe obtain a larger aquarium.

A new color (*new* since 1954, which is a recent development as far as goldfish are concerned): solid chocolate from Indonesia. The Japanese have developed an iron-colored or rust-colored fish. In the USA this fish may be called a *Copper Ribbontail*. The Japanese call it *Tetsuonaga*. ➥

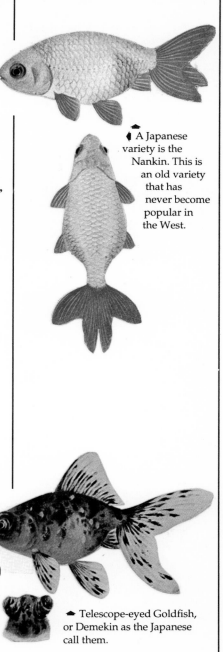

◄ A Japanese variety is the Nankin. This is an old variety that has never become popular in the West.

➥ Telescope-eyed Goldfish, or Demekin as the Japanese call them.

The Common Goldfish

The name of this variety hardly does it credit. It is the original popular little fish from which all other types were developed. In its own right it has many followers and has been bred to a very high standard, both in shape and in the wonderful range and depths of its colors. It will attain a length of up to 25cm(10in) in ponds but in an aquarium it will never reach anything like this length. All goldfish will only grow to a length proportionate to their living area and to the number of other fish present. There is a Japanese form which has a double tail and is called the Wakin.

▲ This is a Japanese variety of goldfish called a *Watonai*. It has an elongated body and a carp-like dorsal fin with a split tail.

The Shubunkins

There are two varieties of this goldfish, the London and the Bristol, which were developed in these two English cities. The London is actually the same shape as the common goldfish but is of the nacreous scale type. It has a blue background with patches of violet, red, orange, yellow, and brown spotted with black.

The Bristol variety differs from the London in that it has much more developed fins, especially the tail. This is well forked with the lobes being well rounded. The paired pectoral and pelvic fins

▸ This is a London-type Shubunkin goldfish.

A Japanese type of goldfish called a *Wakin*. ◄

The Oranda is a hooded ▸ goldfish with a dorsal fin. (The Ranchu is the Lionhead without a dorsal fin.)

are ample without being excessive. Color is as in the London variety.

Comet

The Comet is a very streamlined goldfish that is best seen in large tanks or a pond, where it can fully display its lightening bursts of speed. These are possible because of its long and

▲ This is a cross between a Wakin and a Ranchu. It is called a *Kinransi* in old Japanese.

deeply forked tail. Its other fins and body shape are similar to those of the common goldfish. Developed in the USA, it is hardy and popular.

Lionhead

This variety has the hood of the Oranda but its fins are much smaller. The tail is divided while the dorsal fin is missing altogether. The Japanese form has a downturned caudal peduncle (the body area from which the tail grows) and is called the Ranchu.

◀ The Chinese goldfish are more easily distinguished from Japanese and American goldfish by their anatomical distortions. The Chinese describe six head types (high head, tiger head, goose head, lion head, toad head and rat head). They have seven eye types, several scale types, and many color types. One of the more attractive forms developed by the Chinese are the Lionheads. These are hooded goldfish (*hooded* meaning a growth on the head) which have no dorsal fin. The photos on this page show the various kinds of Lionheads commonly available in your pet shop. More exotic varieties are available. The ideal characteristic is to have a smooth dorsal profile with no hint of the base of the missing dorsal fin.

Veiltail

This very glamorous variety sports long trailing fins, that of the tail being wide and square cut. The dorsal fin rises high over the egg shaped body. There is a telescope eyed variety in black which in known as the Broadtail Moor. Like all black goldfish, many lose intensity of color as they age, when they become somewhat brassy on parts of their body. This and the flowing varieties must be considered more delicate than those previously discussed, so watch that water temperatures do not drop too much in unheated homes during the winter months. The Globe eye variety is similar to the Veiltail but has a forked tail and the eyes are on truncated appendages not on spherical ones.

◄ The ideal Veiltail goldfish has long, flowing tail fins. We use the plural *fins* because they have two tails and both must be equal in size, shape and color. This variety was developed in Philadelphia and this illustration came from a Philadelphia publication of 1917.

◗ When a Veiltail has the imperfection of having its divided tail fin united, it becomes a 3-pointed tail which has many names, such as *Nymphs*, *Hukinagashi*, or *Bannertail*. Whatever the name, these are inferior fish. If you keep them outdoors, they must have a shallow pool as their swimming is impaired by the imperfect tail fin.

◗ Veiltails have been developed in the USA with additional features such as narial bouquets (Pompon), cranial caps (Orandas), bubble-eyes, and even, sometimes, more than one of these characteristics.

Fantail

The main features of this more exotic variety are the egg shaped body and the well developed fins. It is available in all selfcolors, variegated (mixture of colors), and as a calico. It may have normal eyes or those that are telescoped, which means on the end of fleshy appendages. The Japanese form is called the Ryukin and has a pronounced hump on the back. They are hardy and suited to aquarium or pond.

☛ Japanese fantails have an egg-shaped body like the one shown here. Chinese fantails have an additional hump on the back to make them more rounded. American/English fantails are merely veiltails that have shorter fins.

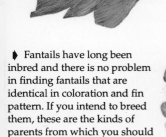

◗ Fantails have long been inbred and there is no problem in finding fantails that are identical in coloration and fin pattern. If you intend to breed them, these are the kinds of parents from which you should choose.

☛ All goldfish spawn the same way. The male chases the ripe female, bumping against her until she releases eggs which he randomly sprays with his milt. The eggs are adhesive and stick to anything they touch *once they are fertilized*...until being fertilized they are not sticky. The two photos above show fantails spawning.

☛ Sometimes fantails have throwbacks to poor quality *Comet* goldfish. These have a single tail fin and normal dorsal fins.

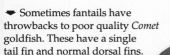

▶ The Oranda is called the *Shishigashira* or lionhead in Japanese. It features very long, elaborate fins and a hood or cap that should not reach below the eyes. The Chinese have developed an Oranda with a red or strawberry cap. These have many names. The usual name is *Red Cap* or *Hong Kong Redcaps*.

▶ If the body color is not solid, the Oranda can take the name of the color type like a calico oranda.

The ultimate in beauty may be the *Pearl Scale Oranda.* ◆

Oranda

This variety has a wart, or raspberry-like growth on its head known as a hood. It otherwise resembles a Veiltail. Available in all colors, the nacreous form is know as the Azumanishiki. Those in silver with a red hood are called Redcap Orandas.

A *Pearl Scale Oranda* with a shallow cap rather than a ◆ lionhead.

Other Varieties

Among the more delicate varieties of the goldfish are the bubble-eye, where the eye is situated on the end of large fleshy balloon-like growths that sway about as the fish swims. It also has no dorsal fin. Then there is the Celestial where the eyes face upward on telescope appendages. They are normal when the fish is young. The Pompon sports much developed nasal septa, which are the nostrils. They are very fleshy. Again there is no dorsal fin. The Pearlscale is so named for its domed scales. Its fins are similar to the Fantail while the body is egg-shaped. There are many other varieties that are often known under their Japanese names. These are rarely seen in pet shops and are very much the forte of the specialist. They require careful management and many are often kept in their own small aquariums. You would need to purchase one of the large goldfish books to read in more detail of these varieties.

▶ A Pearlscale Oranda.

▶ A Telescope-eye Goldfish.

A Water ▶ Bubble-eye Goldfish.

➤ A Black Moor Telescope-eye Goldfish.

▶ A Celestial-eyed Goldfish...always looking at heaven.

The growth on a goldfish's head is not enough to determine its name. If it has a growth and a dorsal it is an Oranda; without a dorsal it is a Lionhead. But this black goldfish also has a beard!!! Actually it is a growth like the narial bouquet...such a fish has no name as yet. Perhaps Bluebeard might be apropos?

A Pompon pair without a head growth.

A Pompon with a head growth and a dorsal which makes it an Oranda Pompon. The word *pompon* is French and refers to the rounded tassel on the top of some knitted hats or berets.

A growth around the head with absolutely perfect narial bouquets makes this a perfect Pompon..and in the rare Rust or Cooper color, too.

This is a young Ranchu Lionhead with growth of the hood just developing. The growth will be red, which the Japanese call the Tancho. The word *tancho* derives from the stork of Japan which has a red spot on its head...as does their flag!

This Pompon with the beard is a truly weird looking goldfish. This variety has not been named as yet.

A pretty Pompon Fantail with black fins and a black narial bouquet.

A beautiful Calico Veiltail Pompo

A Shukin Japanese goldfish with narial bouquets is called a Shukin Pompon. This is an albino; note the red eyes.